HIS LIFE AND OUR LIFE

HIS LIFE

AND

OUR LIFE

The Life of Christ
and the Life in Christ

JOHN A. MACKAY

WIPF & STOCK · Eugene, Oregon

Wipf and Stock Publishers
199 W 8th Ave, Suite 3
Eugene, OR 97401

His Life and Our Life
The Life of Christ and the Life in Christ
By Mackay, John A.
Copyright © 1964 by Mackay, John A. All rights reserved.
Literary Agent - John Mackay Metzger
Softcover ISBN-13: 979-8-3852-3305-2
Hardcover ISBN-13: 979-8-3852-3306-9
eBook ISBN-13: 979-8-3852-3307-6
Publication date 9/13/2024
Previously published by The Westminster Press, 1964

This edition is a scanned facsimile of the original edition published in 1964.

To my life companion
Jane L.

Contents

What Is Life?

LIFE is both mystery and achievement. It is a subject for learned research and a fountain of spiritual energy. Leaving to the scientist the study of life in general and to the philosopher that of ultimate being, I will confine reflection in this small tome to the question of human living.

Across all boundaries of culture and race, of political theory and religious thought, the problem of man, the so-called anthropological problem, has acquired transcendent importance. What does it mean to be a true human being? When is a person truly alive? What do real "living" men and women look like? By what marks are they known? How can people in general become the persons they ought to be, if they are to fulfill in the truest sense their human vocation?

This question is all the more important when we consider the situation today. It is current knowledge that an immense proportion of men and women who are designated "Christian" give no evidence what-

9

ever that they are really alive. They may be church-related, yet they fail to relate Christianity to life and to the problems of life. Their religion is no more than a dull habit. They are quite insensitive to any relationship between believing and living. They spend their years with an unsatisfied yearning to be something they are not, and to possess something they have not. They remain totally unaware that there is a dimension to human living beyond anything they have experienced or thought possible but which is nevertheless attainable.

The meditations that follow are primarily addressed to this situation. They aim at answering two basic questions. First, What is the ultimate pattern for the life of man? Second, By what power can a man become truly man and live as a true man should?

The answer proposed for the first question is this: In the historical life of Jesus Christ we discover the essential features that provide man, whatever his country, his culture, or his time, with the true pattern for living. The answer to the second question may be expressed thus: When man takes God seriously, God supplies him with the needed power to live in accordance with the divine pattern for human life, so that his life becomes vibrant with the life of God.

Let me set these affirmations in due perspective before passing on to clarify them in detail.

Prologue

THE PATTERN FOR LIFE

The time has come to rediscover and take seriously the true humanity of Jesus Christ as the pattern for human living. A crucial need of our generation is that people everywhere, Christian and non-Christian alike, should see in the New Testament portrayal of Christ the essential principles and attitudes that should determine the quality of man's life.

For Christians it is not enough to extol the "Christ event." Nor is it sufficient that they entertain a high view of Christ's person and redemptive work. The imitation of Christ, at present so disdainfully slighted, must be seen in a new perspective and become normative for Christian living in the mid-twentieth century.

Involved in this perspective is the rejection of that subtle docetism so common among church people which, by exalting exclusively Christ's divinity, empties his historical selfhood of true humanity and by so doing makes it irrelevant for serious imitation. Equally to be rejected as inadequate is a glowing tribute to Christ's rich humanity that fails to recognize it as the manhood of the God-man in whose perfect humanity God dwelt in his fullness.

There is an ultimate Biblical criterion by which all Christians, whatever their creed, profession, or church connection, must be judged and will eventually be judged by the Judge of all. That criterion is Christlikeness. To be a true Christian, a member of God's New Humanity, a person must of course have committed himself to Jesus Christ as Savior. It is no less imperative, however, that he follow Christ as Lord in active obedience, while seeking day by day to fulfill his Christian calling.

For that reason we will study *his* life as the pattern for *our* life. "The Great Rhythms" in the life of Christ are an attempt to set forth the timeless and dynamic relevancy of certain selected features in the historical life of Jesus of Nazareth for Christian life and witness today. Rhythms are dynamic alternations from one phase of action to another. Each alternation, as it becomes manifest, fulfills what was involved in the phase that went before.

We will accordingly rivet our gaze upon "Jesus the pioneer and perfecter of our faith" (Heb. 12:2). We will take seriously the injunction that Paul addressed to the Christians in Philippi: "Let Christ himself be your example as to what your attitude should be" (Phil. 2:5, Phillips translation). And we will remember, for our encouragement, that Christ is able to "sympathize with our weaknesses," for he, "because of his likeness to us, has been tested every way, only without sin" (Heb. 4:15, The New English Bible).

THE POWER TO LIVE

It is impossible to study the historical reality of Jesus Christ as a pattern for living without becoming aware that he is presented in the New Testament not only as light but as life. He shows man the way to take, and he supplies man with the needed strength to take that way. The Gospels and the epistles abound in references to the inseparable connection between simple faith in Christ and participation thereby in the infinite resources of Deity.

It is a remarkable fact, however, and a witness to the spiritual unity of the Bible, that it is in the Old Testament that we find the most striking pictorial presentations of the power of God in the lives of men who take him seriously. From the time of the Abrahamic adventure, when a retired landlord became a nomad, the reality of God as a source of strength in the life history of people has a prominent place in Old Testament narrative. God's enabling presence glows in the lives of political leaders, poets, and prophets.

In the writings of the great prophet of the exile, we have a classical description, a veritable jewel of poetic imagery and prophetic truth, in which God transfigures the lives of people who expectantly "wait for" him, allowing him to be truly God in their lives. The dramatic experience that becomes theirs when God is their strength is the theme of the three closing studies in this little book.

The seven meditations that follow appeared in their original form in *Presbyterian Life*. "The Great Rhythms in the Life of Christ" were given as Bible studies at a gathering held in Chicago in September, 1962, under the auspices of the Commission on Ecumenical Mission and Relations. They were made available for readers of *Presbyterian Life* during the

His Life and Our Life

Lenten season of 1963. The studies "When God Is Our Strength" were published some years before. With the encouragement and at the request of two cherished friends, Archie Crouch of the Commission on Ecumenical Mission and Relations, and Robert Cadigan of *Presbyterian Life*, the whole series has been carefully restudied and is herewith presented to readers new and old.

It is the deep desire and prayer of the writer that his life, and the life of all who read these pages, may be patterned on the example of Christ and renewed by the power of Christ, till traveling days are done.

His Life

The Great Rhythms

1

From the Dove to the Devil

Jesus' public life began, his vocation as redeemer of mankind was initiated, by a symbolic act. He was baptized in the Jordan River by a God-appointed man, a rugged ascetic called John. "The Word become flesh," the Father's eternal Son, identified himself in baptism with the whole human family, which stood in need of forgiveness and spiritual rebirth.

Upon the head of the newly baptized stranger the Holy Spirit in dovelike form descended. God had sent the Spirit as the seal of his abiding presence with the Galilean in his redemptive mission, and to supply the power needed for the accomplishment of that mission. At the same time words sounded from on high: "This is my Son, my Beloved, on whom my favour rests" (Matt. 3:17, NEB).

I

What was the significance of Christ's baptismal experience by the Jordan? The core of that experience was the acceptance by Jesus of his life's vocation to be the agent of God's reconciling love. By such acceptance he became committed to all that the fulfillment of that vocation might involve. The Christ who accepted his vocation became thereby a pattern for every Christian. His baptism became the pattern for our baptism. Christian baptism has true significance only when the baptized person, at some point in his life, definitely commits himself to Jesus Christ and accepts his vocation as Christ's follower.

To be Christian in a worthy sense, in the only sense that will stand the scrutiny of the New Testament and of "so great a cloud of witnesses" who have gone before, means unreserved commitment to Jesus Christ, who is the Personal Truth. It means to follow in Christ's steps in obedient and joyous service, whithersoever that service may lead.

But Christ's baptism also has significance and challenge for folk in general who are concerned about finding a life goal. Human beings become really alive, their life takes on a new dimension, when they know what they are living for, when they dedicate their lives to something bigger than themselves. Self-centered people are essentially subhuman people, whatever may be their wealth, culture, or social prestige. Men and women begin to grow up and be truly human only when they find something to live for, be it an idea, a cause, or a person. In the words of that great ecumenical pioneer, J. H. Oldham, "Life is commitment."

II

But see what happened to the newly baptized Nazarene! "The Spirit," we are told, "immediately *drove*
him out into the wilderness" (Mark 1:12). Why?
There, in lonely vigil, he who was appointed to re-
deem the world and was anointed with the Holy
Spirit for the fulfillment of his task must needs prove
his worth. He must stand up to the spirit of evil, who
held men in thrall.

Look at this strange but inexorable rhythm from
the dove to the devil, this dynamic alternation from
green banks and a flowing stream to a bleak waterless
waste. It is the rhythmic movement from a thrilling
experience of God's gracious reality to a grim, gruel-
ing encounter with God's rival. The devil, as we
shall see, has an alluring philosophy of life and is
specially interested in religious people.

The poet John Milton, author of the great epics
Paradise Lost and *Paradise Regained,* has often been
criticized for having made Christ's triumph over his
satanic tempter in the wilderness the event that re-
versed the tragedy of Eden and "recovered Paradise
to all mankind." Although it is true that the decisive victory of the Second Adam was achieved by
his death and made effective by his resurrection,
Milton does set in true perspective the crucial importance of Jesus' confrontation with the archenemy
of God and man.

What took place in the Judean desert determined

19

decisively whether the New Man would prove himself to be the true man. The Man from Nazareth and the Jordan won the day. The Man whose life was in the most absolute sense God-centered gave unswerving obedience to the will of God in the fulfillment of his vocation, and accepted heroically all the consequences of his allegiance.

In the temptation experience, Jesus Christ was forced to make up his mind on three ultimate problems of human existence. These same problems confront man in every generation.

III

The first problem is this: What is the status of material well-being in the life of man? After a forty-day period of solitary fasting, Jesus was feeling the pangs of hunger. He was waiting and wondering when the silence would be broken and God would issue a fresh mandate. At what he conceived to be the appropriate moment, the tempter said to him, in effect, "Why do you endure all this hunger and weakness? If you are really God's son, as it is said you are, then avail yourself of the power you possess. Turn these stones into loaves of bread and bring your misery to an end."

Jesus' response was an affirmation that "bread," though the most basic element in material well-being, was not in every circumstance the ultimate necessity. A situation could arise when loyalty to God and his will would involve inevitable physical suffering. In such a case, a person should stand firm and endure hardness for the sake of principle, and, in simple trust in God, refuse relief at the expense of sacrificing truth. Said the Redeemer to the tempter, "Man shall not live by bread alone, but by every word that proceeds from the mouth of God."

Yet bread, let it never be forgotten, is a basic human necessity. Never, indeed, was there so much hunger in the world as there is today. God imperiously calls those who have plenty to share their food and substance with those who have not, or face world revolution as his judgment upon them. The economic problem, however, is not the ultimate human problem, as Karl Marx affirmed it was. But neither is the pursuit of material wealth, at the cost of truth, justice, and personal integrity, the supreme objective of human existence, as many fellow Americans declare it to be.

IV

The second ultimate issue with which Jesus had to deal concerned the place of dramatic self-advertisement in the promotion of God's Kingdom. The tempter recognized Jesus as God's Messiah who had come to reveal to men the power and love of God. He suggested that the surest way in which he could win recognition for himself as one sent by God on a great mission would be by a daring, dramatic stunt performed in full view of amazed spectators. Let him leap down from a parapet of the Temple. God, in fulfillment of his promise, would never allow any physical injury to befall his Chosen One. By making his debut in this way, the Messiah would be duly identified, acclaimed, and followed.

But Jesus had faith that his Father would enable him to win a right to be heard by the people as the Messenger of God solely by what they found him to be in daily intercourse, without its being necessary for him to resort to God-tempting acrobatics. He therefore rebuffed the tempter with these words: "It is written, 'You shall not tempt [put to the test] the Lord your God.' "

Never was this particular temptation more insidious than it is today, in the Christian church and in Christian circles in general. A craving for popularity, glamorous publicity, institutional prestige, and a delirium of aesthetic grandeur are most assiduously used to promote the Kingdom of God. But God's Kingdom is not promoted in that way. It is advanced by individuals and groups who, in virtue of what they are and by what God does through them, win their right to be heard on behalf of God. By incarnating in themselves a Godlike humanity, and by their demonstrated relevancy to human need, they predispose people to listen to their message.

V

The third temptation was the most deadly of all. Said the tempter in effect: "Be a realist. You know that men, wherever they live, whoever they are, whatever they do, are my subjects and live under my control. Acknowledge my status by an act of obeisance, and the world is yours." In a word, Jesus was being asked to accommodate himself to the realities of human life and history. By adopting a secularistic policy of expediency and opportunism, he would be acclaimed Lord of the world, without having to change the world or become seriously involved in its problems.

From the moment our Lord rejected this proposal, replying, "Begone, Satan! for it is written, 'You shall worship the Lord your God and him only shall you serve,'" his doom was sealed. The prince of the world would see to that. Calvary loomed on the horizon. But, by rejecting the demonic offer, the Son of Man won the battle that qualified him for the exercise of his ministry to men. He also won the right to die as the Second Adam, the Founder of the New Humanity.

Today we are tempted to accept human nature, with all its sinful aberrations, as normal and inevitable. We are tempted to bow down in silence or in compromise before the contemporary gods of class and wealth, of racial prejudice, material self-interest, and nuclear power. We are challenged by the divinities of ecclesiastical ambition and political expediency. Let us stand fast, fixing our eyes on Him who despised the shame, and as the "pioneer and perfecter of our faith," won the battle.

2

From the Mountain to the Multitude

IN THE imagery of the Bible, mountain solitude is a place of encounter with God. It was so in Moses' life on Sinai, in Elijah's life on Carmel, in our Lord's life on the Mount of Transfiguration.

Many a time throughout the night's dark hours Jesus remained in the uplands in solitary communion with his Father. At break of day would come the descent from the mountain to the multitude. It was a movement from divine encounter to the human situation; from quiet solitude to the clamor and hubbub of life; from celestial vision to terrestrial agony; from beatific experience on the hilltop to the plight of an epileptic boy and his anxious family on the plain beneath.

It is worth observing that in Christ's mountain experiences, his disciples, if they were with him at all, were present solely as lookers-on. They were prototypes of a host of contemporary Christians. They were sideline spectators who, like so many of their successors in our time, did not understand what is involved in direct encounter with Deity.

From the Mountain to the Multitude

I

Several features marked those meetings of Jesus with the Father Eternal. Rapt in silent meditation, he would ponder upon the divine plan of the ages as it was unfolding, and upon his own place within it. The dramatic presence on the Holy Mount of Moses and Elijah, representing respectively the Law and the Prophets, was a symbol of the dimension of beyondness in which his thoughts were moving.

Conversation followed meditation. Jesus conversed in a quiet, intimate manner with God. We can hear the overtones of the exchange, "Thou art my Father — Thou art my Son." Then for the attention of the excited observers, and for all concerned men everywhere and through all time, these clarion words sounded: "This is my Son, the Beloved, in him is my delight: listen to him" (Matt. 17:5, Moffatt). Here is truth that sings, a veritable holy melody that philosophers and proletarians, preachers and poets, churchmen and statesmen, would do well to ponder and apply.

There was supplication too in Jesus' encounters with God. Once on a mountain alone he besought the Father to make unmistakably clear to him whom he should choose as his apostles, men with the qualities necessary to interpret and carry on his work. And at the decisive crossroads in his career, not on a mountain but in a garden at its base, with three apostles near him who were dozing in slumber, Christ writhed

25

in agony. He yearned to know for certain whether it was the Father's will that he should surrender to his enemies and suffer death, that is, whether the cross, the mysterious "cup," was really a part of God's life-giving plan.

Let this, however, be remembered. For Jesus Christ, meeting God, whatever the place or time, whatever the form or the occasion of the encounter, was never an end in itself. The Founder of Christianity, the Lord of the Christian church, was not interested in emotional thrills as such. Nor was his devotional life dependent on symbols, whether sacred or aesthetic. Jesus' communion with God was spiritual dialogue on the Road, and for the Road. Its import was fulfilled in action, in the realization of a God-given mission. More than anyone who ever lived, Jesus Christ, our Lord, knew the reality of spiritual rapture and ecstasy. His encounter with Deity did not send him, however, into mystic detachment from the world. It sent him, rather, to places where common folk awaited his authoritative word, his healing touch, his gracious transforming presence.

II

I suggest we pause a moment before following Christ into his daily ministry among people. An inescapable question confronts us. What of the "mountain" and its abiding significance for Christian thought and life? Solitary communion with Deity is a timeless imperative for Christians. This is true whatever be the human situation in which our lot is cast. Corporate worship at its best can never be a substitute for the soul's personal encounter with God.

It is imperative to restore in contemporary church life the practice of the presence of God, the reality of the "quiet hour," though it should last but minutes, the habit of daily Bible reading and prayer. As members of a mass society in a revolutionary era, subject to ceaseless motion in body and spirit due to technological achievement, we need, more than humans ever needed before, to listen to the voice of the Eternal in quiet solitude. We need to share with God our personal problems and concerns, and receive from him the light and strength we need. Having done that, we shall be ready, as Jesus was, to face the multitude or to undertake whatever may be, in our varied spheres, "the daily round, the common task."

III

The mountain behind him, Jesus now stands among the people. It is a historical fact that concern for human well-being, at the level of the common man, did not originate in the cultures of Greece or Rome or the Orient. It had its birth in Palestine, becoming manifest for the first time in the words and work of a man called Jesus of Nazareth.

A great Christian layman, Baron von Hügel, once wrote to a niece, "Christianity taught us to care; caring matters most." When true to its nature and its Founder, Christianity produces men and women,

Christlike in spirit and passionate lovers of people, who dedicate themselves to the well-being, both material and spiritual, of their contemporaries.

The influence of the healing ministry to which Jesus gave birth was brought home to me in a vivid manner during a recent visit to the Far East. A prominent Hindu had with great reluctance become a patient in the Christian Mission Hospital of Fategarh, India. There he was cured of a serious ailment. Upon returning to his home community, feeling overwhelmed by the affection and care he had received, he burst out, "There is more healing in the dust of Fategarh than in all the waters of the Ganges."

Here is a similar instance. A group of Burmese Government authorities, members of the Buddhist religion, recently approached the directors of a Christian hospital in Burma. They said to them: "We are willing to give you all the money you need for the development of your work. The reason for our offer is this. We have found that Christian nurses are better than Buddhist nurses." Whence the superiority? It stems from a basic difference between Christianity and Buddhism on the question of caring for people. The great Buddha taught his followers that they should abstain from doing harm to anyone. Jesus Christ, on the other hand, enjoined upon his followers that they should manifest loving concern for all who needed care, their enemies included.

Let Christ's followers today remember this fact. The same Christ who on two occasions fed thousands of hungry people, running counter to the cold protocol of his disciples, is concerned about the agrarian millions in Latin America. These people live in dereliction and have come to regard communists as their only friends and saviors.

The Christ who in Galilee sat at table in friendly converse with people who were social and political reprobates, and who befriended, and changed the life of, a prostitute woman, cannot fail to be concerned in the heavenly sphere over things that transpire on earth. For there are people who vauntingly bear Christ's name, and regard themselves as heirs of the purest Christian heritage, who refuse to favor face-to-face conversation with contemporary "tax-gatherers and sinners" in the political order. In the economic order they refuse to sanction the exchange of life's basic commodities with people whose ideas and attitudes they violently dislike, but who are in desperate physical need. In social relations, in cultural centers, and even in Christian sanctuaries, they refuse to give equal status to men and women, boys and girls, whose skin is black. Christians of this kind deny Christ and make the Christian profession a thing of contempt. Let all such remember that because Jesus Christ is Lord of history, they too, like their Palestinian prototypes, will in due course "have their reward."

IV

But Jesus' concern for people went far beyond healing and feeding and the manifestation of gracious friendliness. The common folk associated him most of all with a view of life which he expressed with an "authority" they had never sensed in any teacher. Here was no mere traditionalist, no purveyor of dogmatic jargon, no voluble chatterer of religious clichés. In picturesque literary style which combined poetry and logic at their best, the Galilean proclaimed to his hearers that true life is life lived under the Lordship of God.

The gospel of the Kingdom of God was central in Jesus' teaching. God and not people's personal egos must be supreme. God's scheme for the lives of men and women, and not their own self-interest, was what mattered. They needed to become new men and women, God's men and women. In many different ways, whether he was speaking to individuals or to groups, Jesus emphasized the necessity of radical, revolutionary change in men's lives and outlooks. Regardless of whether he was understood or not, or taken seriously, he gave startling centrality in his teaching to man's need of being spiritually reborn in order to be truly alive. He made it unmistakably clear that people should turn to God in humble recognition of the wrong things they had done and the self-centeredness of their behavior, with the assurance that God would forgive them. And he added an intensely personal, evangelical note.

Lovingly and insistently, Christ called upon spiritually concerned people to concentrate their gaze upon himself as the Way, the Truth, and the Life, as the one who had the answer to their longings and to whom their lives should be committed. Whatever their background or their job, their problems or their associations, let them "come" to him; let them "put their trust" in him; let them "follow" him.

V

From among the thronging multitude, the Lord of Life chose a small group of followers who should become his "witnesses" in a wider sphere after he himself had passed on. Those men became in a special sense his "friends." A biographer of Christ in the early years of the present century made this very true remark. "Christ's home," he said, "was the road along which he walked with his friends in search of new friends." This is true, and supremely significant for all Christians and Christian churches today. On the highways and byways of Judea and Galilee, Christ founded the Holy Community of the Road. His friends were no mere spiritual elite with whom he consorted in esoteric fellowship. "You are my friends," he said to the founders of the church, "if you do what I command you."

Jesus Christ thus consecrated obedience as the supreme category of the Christian religion. To be truly Christian means to be so committed to Christ as the Lord of one's life that the essence and thrill of living consist in active obedience to him. The community of faith called the Christian church is true to its nature, worthy of its birth, and will fulfill its destiny, upon one condition. In every society and situation where the lot of the church is cast, it must never cease to be pilgrim in spirit and missionary in attitude.

CHAPTER

3

From the Wine Cup to the Water Basin

THE scene of the third rhythm in the life of Christ
was an upper room in first-century Jerusalem.
With the exception of a stable in Bethlehem, that
room is rightly regarded as history's most famous
chamber. Within its simple walls Jesus and his twelve
disciples spent part of an evening together. While
they were dining and conversing, the Lord, as host,
engaged in two acts in rhythmic succession. He instituted Christianity's most sacred rite; he also gave the
future exponents of the Christian faith a most needed
and salutary lesson. With impressive gesture he
moved from a wine cup to a water basin, from sacrament to service.

I

The sacramental rite that Christ instituted in the
course of that evening meal, on the night before his
crucifixion, has several familiar names. Some Christians call it the Lord's Supper, others Holy Communion or the Eucharist. But whatever the name, the

reality is the same. The bread and the wine that the Lord of Life lifted up in his hands and blessed, and thereafter passed around to his disciples, are the symbols of his body, which the day following was to be broken for them, and of his blood, which was to be shed for them. By this simple act he made unmistakably clear that he was to give his life for their life. They, on their part, were to commemorate his vicarious death on their behalf by continuing to partake together of sacramental bread and wine in remembrance of him, their Savior and Lord. By doing so, they would participate in his continuing life and look forward to his coming again. Christ himself would become their life; they in turn would experience his real presence, which would go with them to their journey's end.

What was the disciples' response to this act of Jesus? It is quite clear that they did not understand its significance. In fact, it is hard to exaggerate their utter incomprehension of what it was all about. They were so totally insensitive to the meaning of what Jesus had done that they broke all the rules of propriety. Instead of expressing in holy reverence their indebtedness to him, they became suddenly infatuated with their own importance. A delirium of grandeur seized them. A wrangle broke out among them as to "which of them was to be regarded as the greatest" (Luke 22:24). Who was the natural and undisputed hierarch?

It was at this point and in this atmosphere that

From the Wine Cup to the Water Basin

Jesus rose. Leaving the sacramental cup on the table, he proceeded to fill a water basin on the floor, interpreting his rhythmic gesture with these words, "I am among you as one who serves" (Luke 22:27).

II

How paradoxical and full of irony that the men who participated in the first Holy Communion should have acted as those men did! But what of a multitude of fellow Christians today who are as guilty of incomprehension regarding this sacred rite as were the disciples in the upper room? Their incomprehension, it is true, takes another form, but it is an even deadlier form. Some have transmuted formal participation in the Eucharist into a magical substitute for personal participation in Christ. In one Christian communion the holy bread is used in the Sacrament of Extreme Unction to guarantee an entrance into paradise. In others, attendance at the Lord's Table has become an aesthetic substitute for spiritual worship.

How many fellow Christians, at the close of a Communion service, leave the church sanctuary, where they have not been present since the last Communion was held, feeling very much as people do after attending a theatrical pageant. An aesthetic thrill has taken the place of evangelical devotion. They experience no disposition whatever to offer up their own lives to Christ in obedient service. They have eaten and drunk in an unworthy manner. Failing to discern the meaning of the Sacrament, they became "guilty of profaning the body and blood of the Lord" (I Cor. 11:27). For that reason it was never more imperative than it is today that Christians, before the Communion service, should take seriously Paul's injunction to the church at Corinth, "Let a man examine himself, and so eat of the bread and drink of the cup" (I Cor. 11:28). A contemporary equivalent for the time-honored practice of "fencing the tables," which marked Scottish Presbyterianism in its greatest days, is most urgently needed.

Something else in the church situation today as regards Holy Communion gives deep concern. To the current incomprehension of the meaning of the Lord's Supper on the part of a multitude of Christians this must be added. An infatuation regarding their own status and authority possesses the minds of many members of the clergy who administer this Holy Sacrament. Their imperious mood is the contemporary successor of that delirium of apostolic grandeur that broke out in the upper room.

Let me be specific. Due to arrogant claims on the part of many churchmen, Roman, Orthodox, and Protestant, that the ecclesiastical organization to which they belong is the one true church of Christ, or at least that they are successors of the apostles in a way that ministers of other churches are not, these churchmen adopt, albeit conscientiously, this attitude. They refuse to take Communion from the hands of Christian ministers whose ordination they regard as invalid, or to give Communion to members of churches that they consider non-Christian or less Christian than their own. In this way — I say it with sadness, but with conviction — Jesus Christ is betrayed and crucified afresh.

Could anything be more tragic and ironic than this? Christians deeply committed to the ecumenical movement meet together, confer together, cooperate together, but they cannot partake together of the symbols of Christ's broken body and shed blood! With all the faults and failures of the Presbyterian family to which the writer belongs, it is committed to a high view of the Holy Supper and dedicated to the practice of open Communion. When the Reformed tradition is true to its origin, the Lord's Table is open to all Christians who have confessed their faith in Jesus Christ, whatever be the denomination of which they are members.

III

But let us return our gaze to the upper room. Observe the aftermath of the first Communion. Saddened by the egotistical obsession of the communicants, and moved by the same spirit of self-giving that he enshrined in the bread and wine, the Master assumed the role of slave. Divesting himself of his outer robe, and tucking himself up with a towel, he poured water into a basin. Then, in kneeling posture, he proceeded to wash the feet of those aspirants to greatness. Had they on their part been sensitive to the proprieties of the occasion and observed Oriental custom, one of them would have offered, in the course of the evening, to play the servant's part and wash the feet of the rest. But for any one of them to have done so would have signified his acceptance of inferiority at a time when a mania of superiority had gripped the spirit of them all.

The author of the Fourth Gospel provides an insight into the self-consciousness of Jesus at the moment of the foot washing. We are informed that as his hands grasped a towel to perform the act of a slave, our Lord was aware "that the Father had given all things into his hands" (John 13:3). As, water basin in hand, he moved toward his disciples, he knew "that he had come from God and was going to God" (John 13:3).

Could anything be more truly sublime? The Lord of all did not seek to dramatize his Lordship by grasping a rod to hold aloft as a scepter and then, with imperial mien, summon his disciples to do obeisance at his feet. Instead, he himself bowed down, that he might give attention to their feet. He, who knew that his origin and destiny were both in God, and that his life was that of a transient on the road of time, chose to make clear that the eternal God was never so truly God as when, humanized in the "form of a servant," he became sensitive to the elementary needs of men.

IV

When, therefore, the question is asked, "What is God like?" the answer is, "Look at Christ in the upper room." Understand the meaning both of the wine cup and of the water basin. When men inquire, "What should man be like?" the answer is the same: "Look at Christ." Fix your eyes first on the Christ who gave his life for your life, and allow him to be your life. Then look at the Christ who lovingly performed the lowliest human service, and "let this mind be in you" (Phil. 2:5) as you listen to his own words: "I am among you as one who serves" (Luke 22:27). Not many hours after, the foot-washing servant of the upper room became the "suffering servant" of a judgment hall, a garden, and a cross.

What is the implication of all this? It is brought home to us with dramatic realism that the servant image, being the central image in the life of God's incarnate Son, must become the central image in the life of his followers and of the Christian church as a whole. Indeed, it is not too much to say that the acceptance of the servant image, as the image that alone betokens true manhood and womanhood, is the greatest need of human society today.

A most tragic thing has happened. The tradition of colonialism abroad and a false interpretation of democracy at home have made the servant image unpopular. In the former instance, the association of certain forms of human service with servitude and servility, imposed by imperial masters, has made the very word "servant" taboo. In the second instance, a false equalitarianism in democratic society leads many a person to say: "That's not my job. I am as good as you are. Why don't you do it?" In consequence, many important human services are simply not rendered because to perform them would, as with the disciples in the upper room, appear to denote inferiority.

So, too, within the pale of the Christian church. Churches confront the constant peril of aspiring after greatness. Many churches seek distinction by claiming the possession of some feature that will assure them status in popular opinion, or in the esteem of sister churches. Such features may be the architectural design of a church building, the aesthetic elegance of a church service, the social status of a church's membership, the elaborate organization of a church's life, or even the dogmatic orthodoxy of a church's beliefs. But Christian congregations may possess one or all of these features and be less than true communities of Christ.

V

A final question arises, For what does a Christian congregation exist? It exists to live by the life of Christ, to follow the example of Christ, and, by word and deed, to proclaim the gospel of Christ. Apart from its annual contribution to a mission budget, is a congregation missionary-minded? Have its members Christian zeal? Do they influence or serve the environment where their place of worship is located? Are they unashamedly Christian in their homes, in their business, in their professional life, in their public relations? In a word, do they take seriously that in Christ Jesus, God took "the form of a servant"?

Let us, writer and readers together, ask ourselves this. Are we disposed to allow the servant image to be engraven by the Holy Spirit in our lives? Are we willing, by the grace of Christ, so to live under his Lordship that in reverent imitation our lives shall reproduce the rhythms of his life? In a word, are we willing to follow Christ from the Jordan to the desert, from communion with God to concern for people, from partaking of Christ's cup to filling our basin with water for the feet of fellow mortals on life's road?

4

From the Cross to the Crown

THE final rhythm in the life of Jesus Christ was the rhythm from death to resurrection, from the cross to the crown.

The principal stages in this rhythmic motion are given classical and sonorous expression in the Apostles' Creed. Jesus Christ, God's only Son, our Lord, "suffered under Pontius Pilate, was crucified, dead, and buried; he descended into hell; the third day he rose again from the dead; he ascended into heaven, and sitteth on the right hand of God the Father Almighty; from thence he shall come to judge the quick and the dead."

I

The crucifixion of Christ is the climactic event in the Gospel narrative. Christ crucified occupies the central place in classical Christian theology, in Christian art, and in true Christian preaching. Said the man who was converted to the Christian faith by an encounter with the risen Christ, "We preach Christ crucified" (I Cor. 1:23).

From the Cross to the Crown

There was a Scottish preacher, an eighteenth-century humanist, who, in a sermon delivered from his Edinburgh pulpit, said this: "If only a perfect being were to appear on earth, men would immediately acclaim and follow him." His assistant, a young man of evangelical discernment, preached in the evening. Without direct reference to the morning service, he remarked, "A perfect being once appeared on this earth, and men cried, 'Crucify him.'" This precisely is the great irony of human history. The only being in history who was perfectly human was spurned by humanity at its best. Jesus Christ was publicly and cruelly rejected by the most representative men of his generation.

Here is the tale. Christ was rejected by the leaders of the world's purest religion. The priests and teachers of Judaism were bitterly resentful because the man from Nazareth proclaimed ideas and sanctioned attitudes that they abhorred. They were bitterly resentful, too, because their economic interests, in particular the income they derived from religious graft, were imperiled by things he said and did.

Christ was also rejected by the proletariat. The masses and their leaders were at first enamored of him, because of his sensitivity to human need and the glamour of the acts he performed. But when he refused to accept a political role and be the Messiah of Jewish nationalism they became disillusioned and irate. So in the end they said, "Away with him." He was abandoned even by his closest friends. One of them betrayed him, another denied him, and they all forsook him.

Solitary and alone, the only perfect man who ever lived was ignominiously condemned to death by the representative of the world's most famous judicial system. Pilate, the Roman procurator, agent of Roman justice, allowed himself to submit to the demand of Jesus' enemies. Wittingly, but reluctantly and most apologetically, he sanctioned a judicial murder. Shortly thereafter, Roman soldiers with traditional brutality and more than ordinary cynicism impaled the Nazarene on a cross.

II

But the Crucified became the Conqueror. On the cross Christ initiated his spiritual triumph and began his cosmic reign. How tremendous were the stages of victory! In an agony of physical suffering and the butt of cynical gibes, the Crucified lifted up his voice and prayed, "Father, forgive them; for they know not what they do." No poison of resentment had been distilled in his spirit. No venom of hate issued from his lips. This plea to God following all he had suffered from men signaled the first stage of his triumph. Had Christ succumbed to bitterness, the tempter would have won the day. But the dove defeated the devil. He who had vanquished the Prince of this world at the beginning of his career, winning thereby a right to *live* for men, now, at the end of his career, won a right to *die* for men. He could say decisively, and with deeper meaning than when he used the words the day before; "The Prince of the world . . . has no rights over me" (John 14:30, NEB). On the "rugged cross" Jesus Christ died for the sins of the world.

In the figure of the Crucified, as the darkness descends upon the hill Golgotha, we confront the holy mystery of the atonement, which is also the at-one-ment. Words and concepts fail to interpret adequately the full dimension of the death of Christ. Theories may come and go, but the event remains in all its magnitude and revolutionary significance. The representative of God and man gave his life for men. "God was in Christ reconciling the world to himself." Paul, who wrote these words, put the significance of the cross in more personal terms when he said, "[He] loved me and gave himself for me."

How many millions have become "new creatures," "saved" in the most thrilling sense, delivered from self-centeredness to God-centeredness, experiencing forgiveness and peace, when, in simple trust, they accepted Christ Crucified as God's unspeakable gift and their own unspeakable Savior. In Grünewald's famous picture of Christ on the cross, John the Baptist stands nearby in rugged garb, with his long, curling finger pointing to the Crucified. From the lips of the Baptizer seem to sound the words that he had spoken beside the Jordan River three years before, when he identified to his followers the Man from Nazareth,

"Behold, the Lamb of God, who takes away the sin of the world."

Christ crucified, the conqueror of sin, was soon to become the conqueror of death. The Spaniard Miguel de Unamuno, in his poem "The Christ of Velázquez," which is the greatest poem in the Spanish language, rivets his gaze upon the Crucified and says, "Thou didst save death. . . . Thou madest Death our Mother." In Death's dread womb, a New Humanity was born. Because Jesus died and rose again from the dead, man's traditional and fearsome enemy took on a maternal countenance. Christians whose eyes are on the Crucified can greet death with a smile. They can even hail it with a voice of triumph, "O death, where is thy sting?" For Christ made "death's dark vale" the gateway to eternal life; and suffering has become the medium of life's renewal.

III

Christ's crucifixion and burial were followed by his resurrection. "The third day he rose again from the dead; he ascended into heaven." The Crucified One became the Risen One, the harbinger and firstfruits of a New Humanity, the head of a great body of men and women who came to be called the church.

It is of momentous significance, and is profoundly symbolical, that the first person to be greeted by the risen Lord was not one of his pretentious friends of the upper room but a lonely and loving woman who had lost her virginity. This woman, Mary Magdalene, had met Jesus on one of his journeys. Following that encounter, forgiven and changed, she became passionately devoted to the One who had opened to her the portals of a new life. Christ had become her all.

At daybreak on the third day after his death, this forlorn female stood in anguish at the entrance of the tomb, seeking his body. When a person she first thought to be the gardener said, "Mary," with a familiar accent, a new day broke for Mary of Magdala. A fresh passion was kindled within her. It was to this onetime "woman who was a sinner," the representative of human millions who are in passionate quest of purity and peace and something to live for, that Christ revealed himself first when he rose from the dead. In the spirit of a woman from rural Magdala and of a man from urban Tarsus, called Paul, to be authentically Christian is to be able to say, and to put into practice what one says, "I have one passion in life, and it is He."

IV

From viewing Christ's encounter with the Magdalene at an empty tomb, we pass to a mountain in Galilee. There he who some weeks before gave to his disciples the symbols of his death and continuing life, and later washed their feet, now gave them their instructions for the road they were to traverse as his messengers.

On that Galilean hilltop the risen Lord proclaimed the central objective of the Christian faith and the world mission of the Christian church (Matt. 28:16–20). The Christ who had died to reconcile the world to ,God commissioned his disciples to be ministers of reconciliation. It would be their mission and that of their successors to be his witnesses, to preach the gospel of the Kingdom to all peoples, to summon them to become his disciples and members of a world fellowship of faith. In dedicating themselves to this mission, they were to be inspired by the knowledge that "all authority in heaven and on earth" had been given to him (Matt. 28:18). The Christ who had on previous occasions, and in a mood of equally tense awareness of his status, summoned them to a fellowship of the yoke (Matt. 11:27–30), and later to a fellowship of the towel (John 13:3–5, 14–17), now called them to a fellowship of the word.

As members of the fellowship of the word, the disciples were to become pilgrims and crusaders on the Road. Headed for the *oikoumenē*, the uttermost bounds of human habitation, they and their successors were to fulfill the ecumenical mandate of the Lord. Those who accepted the word were to be baptized "in the name of the Father and of the Son and of the Holy Spirit," and so would become members of the fellowship of the church. The converts were also to be instructed regarding their obligation as disciples of Christ to be obedient to all his instructions.

For this triple task of evangelism, the establishment of new churches, and Christian education, those who accepted the great commission were assured of Christ's personal presence as their road companion, "to the close of the age" (Matt. 28:20). The infant church was thus assured that the Real Presence was not to be limited to the occasional observance of a sacramental rite; it would be an abiding reality for all who trod the missionary road. Let this not be forgotten in the mid-twentieth century by Christians and the Christian church: We can be true to our calling and recipients of the full grace of Christ and of his abiding presence only when we are missionary in spirit and purpose. And this we become when our frail lives are endued, as were the lives of the first disciples, with the Holy Spirit, "who proceedeth from the Father and the Son."

V

There is something else that no Christian dare forget. The Risen One has never ceased to be the Crucified One. Christ is presented in the Apocalypse as the Lamb before the throne who continues to bear the marks of his suffering. His love agony still continues though he is the crowned Lord of all. With his usual deep insight, that great scholar and saint, Blaise Pascal, once said, "Christ will be in agony till the end of the world." In similar vein the eminent Christian philosopher Søren Kierkegaard, having in mind the human situation, said truly, "Perfect love is perfect sorrow."

So must it ever be with Christians and the Christian church. Let love agony for humanity, inspired by the constraining love of Christ, mark our lives. Let us identify ourselves with Paul in coveting that intimate knowledge of Christ whereby an experience of the power of his resurrection serves to equip us to share the "fellowship of his sufferings" (Phil. 3:10). Christians are called to "bear . . . the marks of the Lord Jesus," to endure suffering for his sake until traveling days are done, "until the day break, and the shadows flee away," until "the kingdom of the world has become the kingdom of our Lord and of his Christ" (Rev. 11:15).

Christ Crucified and Risen, let it never be forgotten, will have the last word in history. He is the Hope of the World; he is the Light of the World. In an age of universal history, finality belongs to him. Chanting the words of the seraphic chorus that is sung at Easter time, let us exultantly proclaim, "He shall reign — for ever — and ever — and ever."

Our Life

WHEN GOD IS OUR STRENGTH

5

The Rapture

CENTURIES before Christ, a great Hebrew prophet spoke these thrilling words: "Even youths shall faint and be weary, and young men shall fall exhausted; but they who wait for the Lord shall renew their strength [that is, shall change their strength for God's strength], they shall mount up with wings like eagles, they shall run and not be weary, they shall walk and not faint" (Isa. 40:30–31).

A moment comes when human resources fail and men reach the end of their tether. That moment comes equally in the life of persons and of peoples. When it arrives, the very best of men, men who would ordinarily manifest the glow, the vision, and the robust energy of youth, fail and falter. With a sense of utter futility and frustration they "throw in the sponge."

But no human situation is hopeless if God is taken into account. Even when things are at their lowest and the prevailing mood is one of cynicism or despair, quite ordinary people for whom God is God can rise above the bludgeoning of circumstance; they can prove themselves superior to conventional standards and accepted possibilities.

The man who takes God seriously becomes more than a mere man. By allowing God to be truly God in his life, by saying in all modesty and humility, "Thou art *my* God," he has a source of strength and a quality of life that are more than human. God is his strength, and that makes the difference. Frail, fickle, human effort is transformed into divine energy. A plain man is transfigured. He becomes God's man, a man at his truest and best. In the inspired imagery of the prophet, he who changes his strength for God's strength soars aloft like the king of birds. He runs unweariedly, like a well-trained athlete. Calmly and fearlessly, like a seasoned pedestrian, he keeps on walking to the end of the road. There is in the Christian life this divinely constituted sequence — a rapture, a race, and a walking pace. Each of these phases of spiritual development is unique while all three are intimately related.

I

The first manifestation of God-given energy is of the nature of a rapture, an uplift. It resembles the soaring flight of an eagle, or, as one would envisage it today, the surging takeoff of an airplane from the runway. "They who wait for the Lord . . . shall mount up with wings like eagles."

The experience of spiritual uplift is associated in

the Bible with a sense of God's forgiveness. It is linked to what, in the Apostles' Creed, is called "the forgiveness of sins," that glowing sense of liberation which ensues when a burdened, depressed human feels lifted up toward God, for whom he has longed and waited. The man whose sins are forgiven experiences inward release; he achieves, in the fullest sense, beatitude.

Nowhere in the literature of the Christian church is this rapturous release, the sense of spiritual liberation that follows the forgiveness of sins, so dramatically portrayed as in Bunyan's great allegory, *The Pilgrim's Progress*. Here is the passage. The Pilgrim, we read, all doubled up because of the heavy load he carried on his shoulders, came to a certain highway, fenced on either side by a wall called Salvation. "Up this way, therefore, did burdened Christian run, but not without great difficulty, because of the load on his back.

"He ran thus till he came to a place somewhat ascending; and upon that place stood a Cross, and a little below, in the bottom, a Sepulchre. So I saw in my dream, that just as Christian came up with the Cross, his burden loosed from off his shoulders, and fell from off his back, and began to tumble, and so continued to do, till it came to the mouth of the Sepulchre, where it fell in, and I saw it no more.

"Then was Christian glad and lightsome, and said, with a merry heart, 'He hath given me rest by His sorrow, and life by His death.' Then he stood still awhile to look and wonder, for it was very surprising to him that the sight of the Cross should thus ease him of his burden."

As in the great tradition of evangelical religion, so here: "The wondrous cross on which the Prince of Glory died" became the source of a mysterious influence. The radiation of light was followed by the communication of power. "Christian," we are told, "gave three leaps for joy, and went on singing:

" 'Blest Cross! blest Sepulchre! blest, rather, be
The Man that there was put to shame for me!' "

No longer the earthbound, weary trudge, but three leaps into the air. No more the grip of dark depression, but a melody. The Pilgrim had encountered a reality that gave him insight and strength. He had found a truth that validated itself in his life not by the cold logic of rational cogency, but by the warm power of spiritual liberation. He found a truth with a lilt, a reality that set his heart asinging. In this way he attained that exuberant joy and peace which millions of human spirits long for, which thousands of psychiatrists seek to produce, and which the Christian gospel alone can bestow. In "a look at the Crucified One," Bunyan's Pilgrim found God and a new selfhood. He became God's freeman.

The man from Tarsus, who was one of Bunyan's spiritual masters, affirmed exultingly that those who experienced liberation through the cross "rise" with

The Rapture

Christ. The same power that raised Jesus Christ from the dead lifts them into a new spiritual realm. This realm Paul describes as being "in Christ," or "in the heavenly places in Christ." God becomes in a very real sense their dwelling place, their soul's true home. "Seated" in the heavenly sphere, they enjoy communion "with the Father and with his Son Jesus Christ."

Paul's most classical expression of this experience is the rhapsodical outburst in his great letter to the Ephesians. This sublime rhapsody (Eph. 1:3) is the key to the whole letter. It is comparable, as has been suggested, to "the overture of an opera which contains all the melodies that are to follow." Listen: "Blessed be the God and Father of our Lord Jesus Christ who has blessed us in Christ with every spiritual blessing in the heavenly places." It is precisely this rhapsody, with all that it means for thought and all that it holds for life, that Christians must recover in this grim time. The truth we need is truth that lifts us, truth that sings in us, truth that leads us to the "secret place of the Most High," to that "place of quiet rest near to the heart of God."

II

But the rapture involves *outlook* as well as uplift. It does not end in mere ecstasy. The person who is "risen with Christ" discovers a new perspective for the study of God and man. The "man in Christ" receives, though in lesser measure, such insight into things divine and human as Moses received on the

57

summits of Sinai and Pisgah, such as came to John the Divine in the solitude of Patmos island, and to the disciples of Jesus on the Mount of Transfiguration. Such illumination may come to Christians at the Lord's Table or in moments of secret prayer, as they quietly read the Bible, or listen to the Word being preached. From the perspective "in Christ," God becomes a new reality to the Christian's gaze.

A recent traveler in the Orient was unable during his stay in Tokyo to glimpse the holy mountain of the Japanese because its summit was all the while shrouded in perpetual mist. But soon after his plane soared aloft for Korea, he beheld the snowcapped peak of Fuji in all the glory of the morning sun. So too the Christian, risen with Christ above "the encircling gloom," beholds the splendor of God.

No one whose experience is limited to the natural world of space and time with which science deals, or who passes his days in the narrow academic sphere where the categories of reason hold exclusive sway, has any conception of that vast realm which is the native home of faith. It is in this region, however, and only in this region, where any true understanding can be obtained regarding God and his ways. Only here can be grasped the great principles and patterns of God's moral government. For here the Christian is enabled to think not like a mere man, but like a man whose intellect is illumined by the light of Christ. In a new sense he thinks God's thoughts after him; he surveys all things from God's perspective. The Bible becomes a wholly new book to him. Fresh convictions grip him. A true philosophy of life becomes possible for him.

He now knows among other things, that righteousness is more basic than security, that it never pays to be vindictive, that love alone is creative. In the light of God and with God's outlook a man obtains new insights into the human situation, both as historical process and as contemporary reality. No longer is he condemned to think and live in terms of a frog's view of the world. The universe of the frog is confined to its muddy pond. Its outlook is circumscribed by the grass and the rushes around the water's edge. The frog knows nothing of the fields and the streams, the woods and the hills and the great sea that lie beyond its little pool.

How different is the outlook of the bird. The skylark or the eagle, soaring aloft far above the pond with its rim of obscuring rushes, glimpses the vaster world of nature, the river, the plain, and the great ocean beyond. From the perspective "in Christ" wider horizons open up before the Christian. He discovers new clues to interpret the world with all its multiple contours, its labyrinthine paths, and its revolutionary anguish.

III

Two things become apparent to him who views the world from this perspective. He sees clearly that the tragic secret of human life, yesterday and today, is that man, more interested in possessing a kingdom of his own than in becoming a citizen of God's Kingdom, has wanted to be a divinity in his own right. Man has balked at submitting to the eternal God. For that reason he has, time and again, experienced judgment and disillusion. He has seen his outer world dissolve in disaster and his inner world converted into a sepulchral vacuum. For man without God ceases to be man; and the pursuit of purely earthly objectives leads to the abyss. Again the word of Christ shines with meaning as the true secret of life: "Set your mind on God's kingdom and his justice before everything else, and all the rest will come to you as well" (Matt. 6:33, NEB).

From this same perspective the Christian becomes aware of something else. Amid the social wreckage of man's world he sees a society of hope. That society is the Christian church, which is the temple of Christ, the bride of Christ, the body of Christ, the instrument whereby Christ fulfills upon earth his invincible, redemptive will. Despite the sins of the church, notwithstanding the schisms that rend it and the persecutions that afflict it, the Christian church is the "light of the world" and the "salt of the earth." It is a society whose members are summoned to witness to Jesus Christ in every phase of their thought and in every sphere of their life. To the church and only to the church is assured victory at the end of the road, when "the kingdom of this world has become the kingdom of our Lord and of his Christ." This is the one community against which the "gates of hell shall not prevail." All human imperialisms shall lose their power, all human cultures shall lose their luster; but the "City of God remaineth."

The vision of these things garrisons the Christian's heart with a holy, dynamic peace. This peace, which is "like a river," ensures that a celestial rapture shall become in due course a terrestrial race, that outlook shall become outreach.

6

The Race

THE soaring eagle comes down from the heights; the airplane descends to the runway; Jesus and his disciples leave the Mount of Transfiguration for the plains beneath. In like manner they who have been blessed "in Christ with every spiritual blessing in the heavenly places" leave the sphere of pure vision and high communion for the highways and byways of the world.

The upward movement that lifted the Christian soul into the "heavenly places" has a sequel that brings him back again to the paths of earth, there to live his life with new insight and fresh power. For no mortal can or should attempt to live forever in an ecstasy of spiritual enjoyment or of contemplative vision.

Yet the momentum of the flight and the radiance of the vision remain. Above all, God remains, who empowers those who "wait" for him. The man who has looked at things divine and human in the light of Christ is destined to become the servant of God and man on the roads of earth. "They who wait for the

Lord shall renew their strength, they shall mount up with wings like eagles, *they shall run and not be weary*."

I

In the Bible, running is the symbol of a great devotion. The object of devotion may, of course, be very unworthy, for people often "run to evil." It is tragic but true that there are feet which are "swift to shed blood." It is not breathless enthusiasm in itself that matters. There are men, alas, who have said like Milton's Satan, "Evil be thou my Good." They speed over land and sea to convert men to their own likeness, and do it, alas, in the name of Christ.

But the most famous runners in the Bible were inspired by love, not hate, by a pure love passion for God and man. Take a striking illustration. When the father of the prodigal, true image of the Father in heaven, saw his dishonored boy come tremblingly back from the brothel and the pigpen, he *ran* to embrace him. Forgetting his resentment, swallowing his pride, laying aside his dignity, he sped swiftly to kiss the repentant swineherd from the "far country"; for the wretched youth was his own son.

Another example of running inspired by love is the attitude of Paul. The man from Tarsus who had "seen the Lord" and heard "unutterable things" in the heights regarded himself as an athlete in training for the racecourse. An aspirant to honors on the track of life, he subjected himself joyously to the severest self-discipline that he might win the victor's crown.

In manifesting this spirit, Paul ran counter to a popular trend in his own time. Epicurus, the most idolized figure in that generation, was a man who sought to manifest at all times and in every circumstance an "unruffled imperturbability." For this philosopher, passion or excitement of any kind was unworthy of a cultured, superior human. Because of his quality of serene detachment, his contemporaries gave Epicurus the name of "Savior." But a converted Jew from Tarsus, who had seen the risen Christ and heard his word of command, was unashamedly tense and stirred about fulfilling the mission for which Jesus Christ his Lord had called him to his service. "I do not run aimlessly," he said, ". . . I pommel my body and subdue it, lest after preaching to others I myself should be disqualified." (I Cor. 9:26–27.)

> Yes, without cheer of sister or of daughter,
> Yes, without stay of father or of son,
> Lone on the land and homeless on the water
> Pass I in patience till the work be done.
> (From *Saint Paul*, by F. W. H. Myers;
> The Macmillan Company.)

The truth is this. No one can be a real man or a real woman who lacks ardent devotion. Life does not begin at twenty-one, or at forty, or at seventy. It begins when one is captured by something bigger than selfish self-interest — an idea, a person, a cause, to live for and die for. An individual who is living aimlessly or selfishly is not really alive. He exists, but he does not live. That rugged Spanish thinker, master-mind of his generation, Miguel de Unamuno, used to say to the young intellectuals of his country for whom, as for many in the United States today, culture meant complete detachment from life, "Find a great idea, marry it, found a home with it, and raise a family."

We have heard it said, "Fear the man of one idea." The strength of communism lies precisely in this, that communists, inspired by a Marxist philosophy of life, are passionately committed to certain fixed ideas, whereas the members of many a democratic society are unacquainted with the ideas and the loyalties by which alone democracy can live. "No heart is pure that is not passionate, no virtue is safe that is not enthusiastic." So wrote a prophetic thinker in the staid Victorian era. Passion must be met by passion; a demonic passion must be driven out by the strong expulsive power of a pure affection. In this volcanic, revolutionary time when millions of souls are on fire, flamingly committed to ideas and causes that are not related to God's Kingdom, it is time to rethink the place of passionate commitment in the Christian church. For the victory is to be won by one fire or another, by the fire that devotion to purely material interests can inflame or by the fire enkindled by the Spirit of God.

II

The supreme devotion, the purest and most transforming devotion, the devotion that restores human nature to God's pattern, is devotion to Jesus Christ and his Kingdom. When a man is mastered by an awareness of the debt that he owes to Christ, and can feelingly say with Paul, He "loved me and gave himself for me," he begins to "will one thing." Life has a new impulse, a new soul. A chant is born. "To me to live is Christ," which is to say, "Life means Christ to me."

This devotion engenders a sense of mission. It has carried some Christians beyond the frontiers of their native land to "preach the gospel to every creature," to "make disciples of all nations." It has led others to initiate or support some enterprise related to God's Kingdom in the homeland. Whatever be the particular form of missionary interest or devotion, whether it be in the realm of thought or of life, and whatever the land or sphere in which it is expressed, what inspires the frontier spirit is the sense of belonging to Jesus Christ, who is at once the Truth and an ardent lover of men.

Christ taught men to care. That was his supreme contribution to human culture. He taught men to love, to be concerned about people who were not naturally lovely or lovable, people who had no special claim upon their interest and were not in a position to recompense their benefactors for kindnesses bestowed.

For all too long the word "love" has been associated with pure sentimentality. As a result, moreover, of a certain type of novel, of a certain type of motion picture, and even of a certain type of psychology, there has been attached to love a stigma of low passion and licentious lust. The present crisis of human society is preparing the way, however, for a restoration of the concept of love to its pristine dignity and its incomparable power.

This bears directly upon the current situation in the Christian church. Without missionary ardor no man can be a Christian in the full sense, however devoutly he may worship, and however successful he may be in maintaining high standards of ethical behavior. The glow of worship must lead the Christian beyond the precincts of the sanctuary; the truth of doctrine must give him interests beyond the arena of theological debate. Worship and theology must arouse his concern for the "crowded ways of life" where men sin and suffer, where they need to hear the gospel of forgiveness and of reconciliation and of transforming power, where Christian enterprises need to be launched or are languishing for lack of support.

III

In the secular realm of culture and civilization, ardor born of Christian love is desperately needed. No matter how much technical skill an educated person may possess — even though his brain be a library of encyclopedic knowledge — if he is incapable of true love and does not manifest genuine concern for others, he has no contribution to make to the main cultural problem of our time.

Our cultural problem consists in this: Educated people must succeed in establishing brotherly relations among themselves; they must radiate friendliness across the frontiers that now tragically separate the diverse groups and nations of mankind. If contemporary education is unable to produce friendly spirits, we have reached the end of the cultural road, and no amount of knowledge or skill can save us. More than that, unless the leaders of mankind in the international sphere find a way to create friendship and take full cognizance of the political power of forgiveness, there is nothing but gloom in the time ahead. The only thing that can create true culture, the one power that can create a genuine civilization, is that men and women everywhere should learn how to care for one another, to forgive one another, to seek the good of one another.

IV

A word is called for about emotion in religion. It has become fashionable in many church circles, especially in the great traditional churches, to look with profound suspicion upon every manifestation of deep religious feeling. The naturalness of emotion in all other realms of human experience is admitted, and its expression, in appropriate circumstances, is expected and even promoted. But in religion, profound feeling that engenders missionary zeal is regarded as a perilous intrusion into the conventional proprieties of church order. A great enthusiasm is frowned upon as a disturbing thing. A cult of Christian sedateness has developed. Liturgical procedures are promoted whose aesthetic perfection sanctifies spiritual death. And yet how much there is in the Christian religion to get excited about!

On the other hand, the danger inherent in emotional ardor is apparent. We have seen it in these last times in movements that were inspired by "truths gone mad." We have a right to fear the emergence, and still more the predominance, of fanaticism within the Christian community. And yet it is oftentimes very difficult to separate fanaticism from faith. We are constantly confronted with this dilemma. How shall we secure that everything be done "decently and in order," in the common life of the Christian community, while recognizing that fanaticism is of the lineage of faith? We would do well in this connection to heed the sobering words of Arnold J. Toynbee, the historian. Upon the basis of a profound study of human civilization, Toynbee bids men beware lest they "stifle fanaticism at the cost of extinguishing faith."

This is precisely the predicament in which contemporary Protestants find themselves. We have frowned upon all manifestations of emotion. We have become fearful of chain reaction in the realm of feeling. We have convinced ourselves that the staid, conventional, kindly person who balks at the expression of strong spiritual exultation or depression is the normal Christian type. This type we would universalize throughout the globe and hail as the true ecumenical Christian.

V

From time to time this neo-Greek mood suffers a rude awakening. Our Christian Grecians are confronted with the fact that there are human situations so desperate, and human beings so far gone in sin and misery, that they can only be dealt with by people whom conventional Christians despise. Yet those despised people are able to bring to bear upon their spiritual task such strong faith in God, and an emotional approach so overwhelming, that degraded human lives are transported out of the gutter in which they grovel and begin to conform to a highly spiritual pattern.

As persons who profess to be religious are we concerned that no great devotion has ever gripped us? Do we want to let ourselves really go on the Christian Road? In the Revised Standard Version of the Bible some words of an ancient bard of Israel take on fresh meaning, "I will run in the way of thy commandments when thou enlargest my understanding!" (Ps. 119:32).

Larger vision, truer insight, is our need if we too would run and give ourselves unweariedly to the pursuit of large objectives. Something else also we need. We need to rediscover what it means to "wait on" God, to take him seriously, to allow him to become God in our lives. When we do that we shall experience divine strength. The truth of the prophet's words will be validated afresh: "Even youths shall faint and be weary, and young men shall fall exhausted; but they who wait for the Lord shall renew their strength, they shall mount up with wings like eagles, *they shall run and not be weary*."

7

The Walking Pace

IT is not by chance that the greatest figures in the Bible were great walkers. Abraham and Moses trudged many a mile in search of a country. Jesus Christ and Paul his apostle, after initial periods of retirement from the world, lived upon the road till their work was done. Their stopping places were by the wayside as they moved forward to some place beyond. Only prison and death brought their wayfaring feet to a halt — one in Jerusalem, the other in Rome.

Between his resurrection and ascension, the risen Christ lived moving from one place to another. The encounter on the Emmaus road is an abiding symbol of him who is ever moving "farther." On a mountain in Galilee, Christ promised his apostles that as representatives of a missionary church they would be accompanied by him to the last frontier, "Lo, I am with you always, to the close of the age." He still goes marching on. For that reason "they who wait for the Lord . . . *shall walk and not faint.*" An invisible road Companion walks beside them.

The Walking Pace

It is clear, therefore, that to walk is not an anti-climax to soaring and running. In fact, to be able to "walk and not faint," to maintain the steady gait of the pedestrian, is the crowning glory of Christian living. More spiritual strength is needed to keep a Christian walking with a stout heart in a situation where dullness takes the place of drama, than is needed to lift him upward, or to keep him running till he completes a special task.

I

There are several reasons for affirming that the walking pace is the climax of all that is involved in the rapture and the race.

To begin with, this is *the pace of personal communion.* God is sometimes represented in the Bible as riding a cherub or moving on the swift wings of the wind. He can speak to man in the swirling hurricane, but he also "walks" at eventide in the quiet of a garden. Enoch, we are told, "walked with God." So too in Christian experience. Many a Christian, at the close of a day, or at the end of a period in life, has reechoed the words of those men who walked to Emmaus in the company of One they did not know. "Did not our hearts burn within us," they recollected afterward, "while he talked to us on the road, while he opened to us the scriptures?"

A famous school of philosophers in ancient Greece was called the Peripatetic school. It is as we walk, solitarily or together, that the greatest thoughts often come to us. How many memories come back to life partners, now aging, who, as young lovers, walked hand in hand through dell and woodland, while heart spoke to heart and vistas opened up into the future.

He, moreover, who would win others to the allegiance of Christ must be prepared to walk beside them as they walk, however rugged and hard the path may be. He must win a right to be heard by them; and this right he wins as they come to know him as a wayfarer who trudges beside them on the road and shares their problems. Why should people listen to mere talkers?

II

The walking pace is also *the pace of inescapable duty*. It is the pace of "the daily round, the common task," the pace at which one fulfills one's life vocation. It is the unglamorous pace of dogged devotion.

It is no exaggeration to say that some of the greatest saints in Christian history have been saints of the kitchen and the workshop, saints of the classroom and the office, the clinic and the farm. They are the saints of "the daily round, the common task." Theresa of Ávila, the most notable of Spanish saints, and one of the greatest women who ever lived, used to say to young friends of hers who balked at lowly duties, "My daughters, Christ moves among the pots and pans."

Beyond the rapture and the race there is the quiet tread, the steady step, the unfailing footfall of those, who with Christ's love in their hearts, his light in their eyes, and his smile on their faces, perform the things that they must do day by day as part of their Christian calling. Many a time, it is true, they are tempted to cry out, "Oh, that I had wings like a dove that I might fly away and be at rest!" Many a time it would be easier and more pleasant for them to take to their heels and escape from dull and unpleasant duties. But to do so would mean to deny their Lord, to abandon a situation when they were needed, to leave unattended people who depend upon their presence and help. So, day in and day out they keep walking.

How many Christians are doing today things they never expected to have to do! They had dreams and visions of being something that they are not, of being engaged in a vocation that never became theirs. Circumstances shattered their plans and blasted their hopes. They found themselves in an unexpected situation where their presence was needed. God gave them the strength to accept what appeared to be their plain Christian duty. They triumphed over circumstances; they won as real a victory as any athlete on the racecourse. They accepted their lot; they transfigured their sphere; and in so doing they unveiled in lowliness the splendor of God. They gave cups of cold water in Christ's name. They visited people whom the whole world had abandoned. They did not "climb the heavenly steeps," they did not listen to the plaudits of spectators, but they unveiled

God in each place where their feet trod. Such were in deepest truth "God's men and women."

III

The walking pace it should not be forgotten is *the pace at which the Christian community is developed*. Under the influence of "tongues of fire," multitudes may be converted to Christ with a certain suddenness. But to grow up into Christ, and to become organically related to the Christian community, is a process — quiet, steady, and continuous. Revolutionary change, the attainment of definite objectives by special effort, must be followed by quiet, intensive labor. The development of new life, the sanctification of the Christian believer, is a process. A man becomes a Christian through an individual experience. But he cannot remain a mere individual; he must become related to other Christians. This involves a process in which all concerned must walk.

It is not surprising, therefore, that in the Bible the formation of the Christian community, whether figuratively or in actual reality, is closely related to walking. The shepherd walks as he tends his flock. Walking, he leads them through the valley and makes them to lie down in green pastures; or he descends into a deep gully in search of a lost sheep. So, too, with the building process. Nehemiah's men raised the walls of Jerusalem walking hither and thither, each within his prescribed area, while the stones were being laid upon the ramparts of Zion. It is at the walking pace that the "living stones" are built up into a "holy temple in the Lord."

Ecstasy and crusade have their natural boundaries. Christian nurture requires the quiet, steady pace of the walker. It is perilous to try to accelerate an educational process. The church and the Kingdom have their laws which must be strictly observed. People who were swept into the Kingdom on a wave of emotion must be equipped for Kingdom service at the walking pace. It is an interesting and impressive fact that Pentecostal groups throughout the world who have been noted for incandescent crusading passion tend now to settle down quietly to walk, but without losing their zeal.

IV

Finally, it is at the walking pace in body or in spirit that *Christian maturity is attained*. Lonely hours, seasons of awful solitude, can come into a Christian's life. There come times when he may be cut off from friends and human help, or when the presence and help of friends are of little avail. Jesus was driven by the Spirit into the wilderness far from the crowds who witnessed his baptism in the Jordan. Forty days he remained alone in the desert. Alone he faced the tempter, clinging utterly to God and to the word of his Messianic commission. In solitude, he thought through the implications of being the New Man, humanity's representative in the great assault upon the kingdom of evil.

There are times when a torn spirit, suffering from remorse or the frustration of its dearest hopes, gives vent to a cry, "My God, my God, why hast thou forsaken me?" One had never expected to be in such a plight. But in the valley of the shadow, after we have been bludgeoned and humiliated, and in our own feeling forsaken, the words sound, "My grace is sufficient for you, for my power is made perfect in weakness." Then God becomes our strength and we are ready for the road again. The darkness becomes streaked with dawn, the shadows flee, and life is renewed.

V

Such experiences are part of what Jesus Christ meant when he said, "Take up your cross and follow me." The cross in a Christian's life is something that he cannot evade and remain a Christian. He cannot walk around it or leap over it. He cannot delude himself into believing that it does not exist. There it is, starkly facing him: a deed that cannot be undone, a chronic disease, a family bereavement, a business loss, persecution for Christ's sake. To be loyal to his Lord he must accept his cross and walk life's road with it. But when he does so, something paradoxical, something transfiguring, happens. The heavy, painful cross lifts the Christian soul upward toward God.

> Nearer, my God, to Thee,
>   Nearer to Thee!
> E'en though it be a cross
>   That raiseth me.

The Walking Pace

There lived in Scotland in the seventeenth century a very remarkable man called Samuel Rutherford. Like Jonathan Edwards in America, Rutherford combined the dialectical power of the philosopher with the mystical passion of the saint. One of the chief treasures in Scottish religious literature is the book of letters that Rutherford wrote to friends from a dungeon in Aberdeen where he was imprisoned for his loyalty to Christ. This dungeon he called "Christ's palace." Writing to one correspondent, he said: "If you take that crabbed tree," meaning the cross, "and carry it lovingly, it will become to you like wings to a bird and sails to a boat."

This is the paradox of the Christian life. Things that would naturally get us down and flatten us out can become, if we accept them as our cross, the very things that raise us aloft on eagle's wings or cause us to run like a sailboat before the wind. It is often when the Christian is on the road moving at the walking pace, staggering under an intolerable load, that he experiences release. Crucified with Christ, he is of a sudden lifted up with Christ. Committed to Christ, his "feet shod with the preparation of the gospel of peace" and his burden shared with the Companion of his way, he runs and does not faint.

The man who accepts God's strength is thus invincible. In that strength he can literally do all things. But upon one condition. He must "wait for the Lord." He must allow the Crucified and Risen One to become the Lord of his life. Then he will take wings or run or walk, according as his Lord ordains. And the Lord, in ordaining at any particular time the rapture, the race, or the walking pace will have in mind his servant's spiritual good and the advancement of his own Kingdom.

Therefore, let this refrain possess us:

Wait for the Lord;
be strong, and let your heart take courage;
yea, wait for the Lord!

(Psalm 27:14.)